THESE WORDS THAT I BREATHE

KHADIJA MUSTUFA

AURAQ
PUBLICATIONS

Printed in the Islamic Republic of Pakistan.

Printed: September, 2022   Cover Design: @techcanvas1
Edition: 1st
ISBN: 978-969-749-188-9
Price: Rs 1200 PKR, $12 US

www.auraqpublications.com | raabta@auraqpublications.com
@AuraqPublications | @AuraqBooks | +92-300-0571-530
Printed and Bound by *Passive Printers* - www.passiveprinters.com

To Allah the Almighty for being that one star in the sky I believed in.

For being my hope in an era of despair.

To Mama and Papa who taught me how to nourish that hope so it stays alive.

And to myself,

For allowing my heart to breathe when hope wavered

And simmered

And became a minuscule shard of glass

That pricked me every time I touched it.

CONTENTS

UNFURL - DECOMPOSE - REVEAL

This is an ode to everyone I know for real,
To people I think I know but don't,
To people I don't think I know but sort of
know,
People I like believing I don't know but sadly
know
People I pretend to know, but of course, don't
People I don't know and don't wish to know
People I will never know but wish I did
And finally, to people I happen to know but
wish I didn't

I – THE PROPRIUM

"I am but a mortal who lives to please."

THE FALLACY RE CHANGE

So, tell me, where do I buy a charger for my
brain?

The old one is outdated

Ill-adapted to the exigencies of its shattering
plug-ins

And to the last rites of its bloodless
components

The more I charge it

The more ingrate it appears

Not to forget the lethal torpor that constantly
radiates off its edges

Burning everything that gets too close

Even if it's a little embrace from the heart

Or a mere whisper to simmer down

And forgive

It takes nothing of what I offer

Nor is it of any use to me now

I would go down the line for a resell if it
meant getting rid of it

But it seems the burden is mine to endure

The cure is mine to find

The grave is mine to dig if that doesn't work

So,

I am on the lookout for a new charger

Possibly the latest in the market

A new toy to play with

A new score to settle

A new dream to fulfill

Maybe that will commingle the bickering units

Make them whole again

So they can subsist another day

Another month

Maybe a year or two

Given that I don't explode the brain to crumbs with an overcharge

How's that for a new life even?

Silly girl

Silly, silly girl

She is looking for a new charger

*When it's the overcharged battery that needs
replacement*

Silly girl,

Tending to the outlandish, benign façade

When the interior is rusting away.

QUITCLAIM

I am a wasted soul

Shattering beneath a world of dashed hopes
and shunned promises

Beneath a bed of flowers on blazing fire

Amidst a whirlpool of masked love

And inside a cage of self-reproach

Where a jillion fragments of my cadaverous
heart zap my remaining pluck

Where the remnants of my pulverizing mind
offer help

Puny efforts against an ocean of turmoil

Still failing at every attempt

Because it is, after all, insanely human—

Afraid of what the heart contains

So I stop fancying a change within me

End to a war meant only to kill me

Gasping for air, I implore to set me free

To unearth a world of wonders

Of purity and virtue

Of perfection and hope

Of love and abundance

Of people who care

All the while gleaning my chances of survival,

Of becoming my own companion

My only savior

If only to realize there is no way out

Just a murmuring fantasy of sedentary death

Freedom just a world apart

With my soul making the only difference

And for once,

I intend to disown my very self

For once

Just for once

I don't want to be mine.

THESE WORDS THAT I BREATHE

I have functional dyspepsia

I can't digest pain the way normal people do

For me,

It's the gust of wind that sweeps the air out of my lungs

And the words out of my mouth

So when I speak

I speak through my eyes

And eyes only

And this acidity of speech formulation

Burns me

And burns me alive

And brings me back to life

So I can burn some more

When I guide sorrow down my throat

It slips and slurps like alcohol

Or at least I try to believe it works like that

But kills me all the same

Benignly so,

When love barrels through my esophagus

I choke with the hope that burgeons inside of
it

And clogs my trachea

And I keel over with the deadweight

Not meant for me to carry

Among the warning signs of dyspepsia

Is the burning of the affected heart

With a flame so angry

So rapid

So nimble

It enkindles even the hearts that come to
rescue

I debated going to the doctor

For a few cremated globs that once resembled
a heart

Settling,

In the end,

For self-prescribed medicine

A surgery that stitches lips instead of hearts

Refurbishes wounds instead of repairing
them

And an increased liquid intake remedy

That recommends fuel instead of water

A commendable shortcut to my fear of
doctors

But try as I might

To be my own cure

For a disease this colloquial

Failure is a beast that runs after me

Even when my legs hurt

And my heart

And my entire body thumps with so much
running

And I long to stop

Even when I dare myself to stop

Rashly believing the lies of the healthy

When they say fear follows the spooked

My wounded, ensanguined heart keeps
slithering out of my hands

It belly-flops in its own plashet of gore

With the acuate lumps and morsels

That I keep trying to coalesce

With my bare hands

The blood on them shimmering under the
pernicious light of the sun

Appearing as chaste as neoteric joy on a
pristine cheek

Yet as merciless as bad news under the moon

When I reach for those fallen petals of my
heart

They evaporate

And condense on the mirrors of my mind

The drip drip of their surrender

Soaking all the places I touch

And tread

And drink

And dream

As for these thoughts

These thoughts that I breed

And these words that I breathe

Are seeds that I cannot cultivate

In a garden known for infertility

Precious as they may be,

I hoard them all in a jar of the incurables

Plagued with what-ifs and why-mes

I should and I shouldn'ts

I am and I ain'ts

I breathe in their scent every day

But they don't breathe the air that I breathe

They will never know the world as a place
with seasons

And the earth as home for both thorns and
roses

They don't perceive the light that I reap

Only the darkness that I sow

All they want to see is me

A basket case

In the midst of a catastrophe

At the edge of an indissoluble fiasco

Struggling

And surviving

Barely, if I might add

But not winning

They don't see surviving as winning

They laugh when they see me cheer for
myself

And cherish what they call a mere stroke of
luck

I believe them all

I believe my heartache

And my headache

And the soreness of my throat

Caused by all that noiseless screaming

And I drink all the lies they pour into me

Like uncooked soup

And let it cook inside of me

They see me hesitating

And sweating

And fearing

But most of all,

Burning

Burning irrevocably

And they know,

They know

They have done their part.

FLOWER CHILD

My stubbornness is a felon waylaid on the
street

A prank gone wrong on a whim

A cranky old woman warmongering to combat
monotony

Bickering for hegemonic ground

When there is none to be found

It's death lying dangerously close to the
shadows of life

Wheezing on the meager scraps of a
soothsaid victory

And supremacy

Which is nothing if not a bedtime story for
the artless

An entity now clearly never to come

Has my stubbornness by the throat

At the edge of a hill, it once scrambled of its
own accord

Frenetically guffawing at the indiscretion

And the audacity

While trumpeting the tales of my fear

That my ears may hear

Knowing what they cannot bear

It says to me:

'O you!

Who have dispersed the kind

And followed the blind

You who have despised the beloved

And embraced the shunned

A fallacy has befallen your soul

That which your heart refuses to refute

You are but an epitome of unfulfilled hunger

That which respires in the food of others

And of desires running deep down to your
soul

Hoarded from the joy of the cherished

You arc made of lies that taste like rubber
and rubble

And compliments that smell like rotten
seaweed

And when you shove them down your throat

Grudgingly as it maybe

They smolder your tongue and pockmark
your throat

The food in your stomach burns like molten
plastic

And your taste buds turn to ice

That's what happens when you are a country
you don't want to visit

A flower you don't want to smell

A grimy old book you wish no one ever
plucked out of that bookshelf

Because when you look around

All you see are those stars

Comely and adored

Ravenous yet abounding

Flashing all over like mocking smiles

And grandiose existences

Of dreams never seen, but fulfilled

Of aims never set, but achieved

And there you are

The abandoned moon

Flawed and anomalous

Like a miscalculated figure

An unforeseen disaster

An appearance unwelcomed

Bearing a glow

That brings with it

A measly darkness

That turns the oceans into voids

Spring flowers into demon-kissed petals

Chirping and soaring birds into snoring
cowards

And hearts into autumn leaves

That fall

And fall

And fall

Not for you though

Not for you

You better know who waggles the branches

And scourges the bark

So, does it now dawn upon you?

The darkness of your entrails

And the blinding light of your words

That has killed so many

So many to count

Do you now see what went wrong?

What brought you here?

What kept you here?

And why,

Why of all the places

Death approaches you where you first
breathed

And learned to stand on your own two feet

And tip toe so you could see

Higher

And higher

Never below

Never below where you belonged

All along

There are words inside of me

I know they are there

I can feel their shallow breaths in my veins

Their stupor in my heart

Stupid, effing heart

Their fading war in my lungs

I just,

I just cannot feel *them*

If I could,

I would tell my stubbornness

That friend who mediated between hope and
me

The hope that was serrated on the edges

And when I held it

I bled

And bled

And bled

That friend who kept me fighting

Albeit for all the wrong reasons

And with all the wrong people

That friend who was always, always there

Even when I wished it wasn't

That friend who kept saying

'Your time, your time would come'

I would tell her to give up

To give up fighting everyone and everything

Life works in the flip-flop for the perseverant

I would tell her she has tried hating

And hurting

And playing

And slaying

And it has never, ever worked

It's about time she tries breathing

And smiling

And loving

I would tell her to choose what ought to be chosen

And jump on the train

That is scooting with her proprium

I would tell her not being good enough is still enough

And that being enough is a myth

And myths,

Being myths,

Mythify our existence into a holistic competition

A race for perfection that itself is a myth

Then overlooking the amounts of 'myths' I
have used

I would go on to waggle her shoulders

And profess

With all the courage I can muster

'You too are a myth!'

I wonder if this is the time I was promised

If it has come and it has me under the crook
of its arm

If freedom from its own camaraderie

Is what my stubbornness had meant

When it said 'Your time would come'

I wonder if this pulsing ache in my heart is a
pro tem thing

If I can learn to breathe through it

And then breathe with it

Like it's a part of me

I think now I know how people can dish out
their fortune

In bowls made from crystal hearts

That carry veins made of gold

For smiles rarer than life in space

And still be meekly happy about it

Now I know how they can let their necks be
garroted

Or their hearts be arrowed

Or their heads be bulleted

For a mere share in humanity

That dies a little bit every day

When a mother cries for her slaughtered
child

And we put our ears to sleep

When a black bloke gets kicked out of school

On imputations of color scarcity

When a Muslim recites Kalma

And we anticipate death

When wrong is being said

And done

And created

And we put our voices to mute

And sever our tongues

And seal our lips

And wait

Wait for it all to end

Just end

Now I know how they can have nothing

And still seem to have everything

Because it's not,

It's never about who we are

Or what they think we are

Or what they want us to be

It's not about them

It's always, always about us

About the face we want to see in the mirror

Every morning

When light refuses to shine at our side of the
room

The color we want to feel when we smile
under the sun

And amidst the beauteous stars

The scent we want to carry wherever we go

The dreams we want to bestow when we win

And the ones we want to keep when we don't

It's about the story we want to write

And the actors we want to play

When the sky becomes the audience

And the earth our judge

If it weren't too late

I would tell my obliviously fallacious,

Undeniably loyal,

Adamantly choreographing buddy

That I might have to run and hide

And skip and slide

If only to get away from her

If only to hope

And learn

And grow

Without her fog blinding my sight

And her voice caging my voice

And her ropes foiling my flight

I would tell her

I have lived the being in human being

It's time to become.

EPHEMERAL FOREVER

Life is shriveling away from me

Through scintillas of rage

And mephitic globs of delirium

That smolder any crumb of serenity around me

That instill feeble stories about myself into my delicate mind

That implant venomous seeds of self-abasement

And ignominy

That pluck my cronies from me

Like petals wrenched away from their base

Like skin being shredded apart in beastly torsions

Like the sun leaving the world for never to return

My realm is metamorphosing into steppes of contrary poles

Curling on themselves

While I contemplate the choices I have:

Unhurriedly poisoning sanity or outright
death?

A pipe dream of amelioration

Or unyielding dilemmas of the past?

To the right with nothing left

Or to the left with nothing right?

But even as I ask myself, I know the answer:

I can choose to stand still

Unspeaking

Unseeing

Unhearing

To neither move to the right nor to the left

Yes, I can wait

For things to change

And for life to return as slow as it tends to
leave right now

And assume, albeit foolishly,

That it has nowhere else to go

I am home to my life and it is home to me

And we are just a cantankerous, struggling
couple

A lifetime bond of love that is lost

A far-fetched tale of a family

Sundered for not understanding each other

Yes, I can wait

For the fire to calm down

For the burning ice to melt

And for my beloved to come running back to me

So, when I would open my eyes for the first time

After weeks or months or years of tarrying

I will see it

The light that I have lost, smiling at me

And I would say hello with an enchanted hug

And uprear my ears to hear it rejoin with the same fervor

And together we would make a promise

A promise of gratitude and forbearance for the company

For the bond

So yes, I can wait

I will wait

To meet life again

To meet happiness

And love

And a trillion other miracles

My happy ending, I would call it

And it will come,

Not so soon maybe, but soon

And for that, I have my entire life

An ephemeral forever.

MASQUERADE

I wonder if the stories about healing are all a
sham

If they are merely jettisoned advices bundled
in a jar of jam

For people with the last and the first piece of
bread for hope

If it's poison inside a wine carafe

And a warm breath mistaken for a hug

If it's like treating a skin growing over your
skin

With infinite, immortal layers and no flesh

So when you peel it off

It keeps growing

And I wonder,

I wonder

If I will ever get my skin back

If I will ever be able to scrape and scroll my
finger through it

Like it's a newly discovered element

Discovered, not emerged

Always there in the shadows

Mushroomed on an ox laden with

Unpacked shame

Greasy heartbreaks

Wrinkled papers of unwritten sorrow

And a childhood untouched

Always peeking through the transparency of
my pain

Sometimes clawing at the skin I love to wear

The new skin:

A stopgap pair of gloves for when the weather
goes downhill

And takes me with it

Me: a corroded foundation in the deluge of
heart-shaped pebbles

And rain that reeks of a perfume I am allergic
to

I refuse to pay attention

I refuse to pay attention because

Paying attention means listening

Really listening

And listening means allowing my ears

And my eyes

And my nose to bleed the agony

On the floorboards of my surrogate skin

And my mouth to go blind fumbling for words
in the cold

To freeze and fracture with what it cannot
say

I wonder if I will ever be me again

If I will ever meet the people I love in my own
skin

And broach our bond in my own voice

And cuddle with my favorite kids

With a heart that responds to me

And a body that nurtures that heart

I wonder

If someday

My hands

My pleading, bewailing hands

Will be able to pardon me for what I have
made them do

For a mere shard of empathy

Empathy taken as love

Love that was never coming from the
direction I implored in

And embrace the dirt twixt them on my
bloodied uniform

As a testimonial of my war-built hands

And a moral I long should have learned

To never, ever spare a glance in that direction
again

And I hope

With all my teensy-weensy heart

And I hope I am not a fool to hope

That someday

These hands

These self-pitying, unglued hands

Sprawled on the earth for all the love of this
world

Will roll back to their pride

And applaud their own journey.

MY CATERWAULING SILENCE

My mouth is a seething furnace

Triggered by the constant friction

Between the words dissimulating under my
tongue

Bawling and bouncing

For a release not granted

And the inedible words

That my system keeps refusing

Digestion being an uphill battle these days

They all live in there

In aphonic harmony

As if I don't know

The guerilla tactics they use

When my shield is down

As if I don't hear them whisper

The cacophonies of failure

And send them down my esophagus

With the endnote

'You are what you eat'

As if it's not these words that keep me
chained

To a life

That is more death

And trauma unfiltered

So my mouth is where the demons reside

When my heart listens no more

And my brain shuts the door

I am silent

Despite the demons hunting me down

In my own fortress

Despite the fire in my mouth

Cremating my composure

And procreating a chain of words

I dare not say

I am silent

Because I ought to be silent

Because these words

These words that I breathe

Do not give me breath

Because when I speak

I cram all the words I can

In one breath

And still keep talking

And talking

And talking

Until my voice becomes hoarse

With the onerous reality

Of my succorant existence

Because when I speak

My mouth reeks of the love I never received

That makes them all go away

Because when I let these words out

They open a mirror in the faces

Of my people

So they see me not

But a mere shadow of their own calvary

And my voice metamorphoses into a cassette

Intoning the crucibles of their life

And my voice

Is just a sound

A mere whisper

Of the new horror story in town

No one cares about enough to fear

A speech

Deemed devoid of words

Devoid of pain

Despite the wound within

Because when I speak

I don't really speak

And my words are too refined to be mine

So when I speak

They speak too

And when they speak

My tapered silence

Crawfishes into the shell it came running
from

Knowing damn too well

How their voice will always be a little too high

Their words better

And their trauma greater

And if there were a clash

If verbalizing pain was a sport

My silence knows they would always win.

HOURS THAT FLUTTER AND STUTTER

The clock is ticking

The hours are slithering down my hands like effusive water

Loud and ceaseless

They are everywhere

Yet nowhere

Just like my thoughts

In the basket of laundry outside my room

In the sink beside the dirty dishes

In the tumbling pile of clothes in my wardrobe

In the broken crumbs of my sanity

In the heart clutched in my fist to keep it from shattering beyond repair

In the shower

Under the bed

In my breakfast

On the television

Across the road

On the moon

In my eyes when I look at him

And when I long to look at him

The hours

You see

Are everywhere

Yet nowhere

There are twenty-four in a day

Everyday

Inexhaustible

Indefinite

And yet I wonder why I am unable to do all I
want to do

Why,

At the end of the day

I am thirsty for more;

Why,

There is always too little time

For all the books I want to read

All the hugs I want to share

All the love I want to give

All the stars I want to gaze;

Why,

When I am running away from time

I am also running toward it,

And why,

When people say time heals everything

It only freezes

Alive yet so deadly

It muffles my heart;

Why,

If time is really a balm

Does my wound still bleed every day

As fresh as if it were new

And I have to gag myself

And all my other wounds

So they don't scream

So they don't resuscitate

From a grave still under construction

The clock is ticking

The hours are everywhere

And yet there aren't enough of them

To breathe like I am the only person worthy
of oxygen

To smile like the world needs my sunshine

To wander and lose myself in beauty the eyes
cannot see

To renew the hope I lost to tragedy

To remember not remembering him

To forget I ever lost to fate

To forge ahead

Discard the fumes of fancy I once conceived

In a world so deceptive

It conquers your senses

It drags you in

Makes you feel

And dream

And beg

Until all you see

Are the mangled fragments

Of a life you thought would be yours

In a jillion variants of your existence

A life your heart was inclined to wait for

Never mind the years

Only to see it beget a heaven on earth

For those around you

Time

You see

Is a stubborn child

A wacky teen

A cantankerous uncle

What I mean to say is that

Time loves to stand in your way

That time is a master

Who loves punctuality

But is always late

It is that aunt you wouldn't see at weddings

But will always stay a little longer at funerals

And I am tired of people seeing me cry

And wipe tears

That will always spurt back

As if from a broken duct

In the brightest light of the day

During a hangout

Or in the middle of the night

When sleep unfriends me

I am tired of people running back to me

When the sun is mine

And the stars begin to fear me

What I want my time to know is

That I am not very fond of seasons

And of friends who change with them

What I want to tell my time is that

If you are really mine

You had better stay

What I want to tell my time is that

If you are really mine,

Don't give me a part of the sky

Give me all of it!

LAISSER-ALLER

I sometimes envy the sea

And its unrestrained freedom

With wings sprawled over the earth in
beauteous spumes

Bound to nothing

But their lupine, reckless nature

The sun cedes the sky as day falls

The moon takes over in a Cimmerian night

Only to retreat to its lair,

To give back what it once ventured to acquire

And while the two hideous denizens of the
sky

Strife day and night

The sea is the lone master of the ground

Treading back and forth stoutly

Sometimes slow,

Sometimes fast

Rejoicing at the lack of might

To contain its glory

And here I am

Gliding

And smiling

And weeping at the naked shore

To hide whatever piece I can

Of my tingling impotence

And the vulnerable shards of self-hatred

Stitched to my heart like a wound just sealed

But I dare not purge the veil over my heart

Against the sea without a leash

For my agony may dither whatever little
control it has

Finally imparting the excuse it needs

To revolt against the earth

With all it can give

With all it can take.

CREPEHANGER

My mind is a 3D version of minesweeper

A grisly hodgepodge of triggers

A game of inexpiable bloopers

One wrong step

And BOOM!

Game over

One reckless thought

And BOOM!

Game over

I remember playing this game as a child

Back when computers were a thing

And life was really all fun and games

I remember not understanding it

I remember failing

And giving up

I remember deciphering

That the game was more about delaying loss

Than acquiring victory

I remember learning that winning was not important

It was how far I managed to go

Despite the risks

I remember forgetting about the game as I grew up

And as I grew up

I forgot to remember that this game is a part of me

It lives inside of my head

And I still play it

The triggers are my thoughts

The bomb is my anxiety

But as much as I would like it

There is no game over

Only a chain of more triggers

And a BOOM!

That shudders my sanity

While my anxiety is a powerhouse for contumacious brainstorming

A rhapsody of my psychological fragility

A prehistoric blight that found no cure

Because the only cure available at that time

Was to stop finding it

My anxiety is that customer at the
supermarket

Who reads the push sign at the entrance

But still pulls the door

My anxiety thinks it's okay to be there

As long as nobody notices I am there

But still gets offended when nobody notices I
am there

It tells me that he must like me

If he smiles back at me

But maybe not if he smiles too little

A smile too courteous to be poetic

And also not if he smiles too much

Because that would mean I don't make him
nervous

My anxiety wakes me up in the middle of the
night

Telling me I forgot to turn off the stove

Even though I checked 5 times before
sleeping

And twice sent my husband to the kitchen

Just to be sure

The good thing about always expecting the worst

Is that it doesn't always happen

Which is why I am still friends with my anxiety

Because even in all its despair

There is hope

A fifty-fifty chance of beating my thoughts

Like a bunch of minikin stars amidst the vast dark sky

Like getting that small piece of chocolate

At the end of my cornetto

When we are sharing

Because even in all its misery

There are bedtime stories that help me sleep

Telling people about my anxiety

Is like teaching them how to scale a mountain

Except that I am blindfolded

And my hands are cuffed

And I have never scaled a mountain

Except that when I try to demonstrate

My tongue moves like wildfire

So that my thoughts burn away

And I forget what I was saying

Because to teach someone means to first
learn

What it means to be in your head all the time

To learn the triggers

Those send you cascading down the sierra

You took years to overcome

And you hit rock bottom

In a heap of shame

And disgust

When you should have known better

Than to trust your thoughts

When after years of emotional burnout

You could have wrenched the 'feeling' button

From your system

To do the least

And if this wasn't an option

Remember that there is always

That little green bottle your mom keeps for
wild rats

In the kitchen

Because that's the only way to stop the fuss
in your head

Right?

Because 'till death do us apart'

Was always meant for you and your thoughts

Because death is still an existential comedy

You do for your friends

As compared to what kills you every day

I am that dusty, decrepit clock on my
bedroom wall

Whose hands move anticlockwise

And which never really gets fixed

But hangs there all the same

The clock we forget doesn't work

But still scrunch our eyes at

Every time we are late for something

What this means is

That telling people about my anxiety

Doesn't mean they would rear up their ears

And seal their mouths

That they would bring flowers to my grave

And forgive me for what was never my
intention

Telling people about the civil wars in my body

Doesn't mean they would understand

That it's not all in my head

When maybe

All of it is really in my head

And that sometimes

I am not sure what I am doing

Or saying

And I need someone to hold my hand

And remind me to breathe

Which maybe I have forgotten how to do

Lost in years of battle

And remind me to keep believing in my sanity

To keep tethering myself to scraps of it

Even when my arms begin to scream

To let go

Even when sanity becomes just an echo in
my soul

A lost brother

From another mother

Even when the doors of madness

That I have held at bay for so long

Swing open with a gust of wind

That sweeps me off my feet

And casts me to the ground

Assuring me

That what has begun

Is really the end.

SCIAMACHY

I feel everything

From the heartbeat of the insects under my
bed

To the warm, ethereal smile on my mother's
face

And the pain she believes she can hide

I feel the defeat in the sound of the waves

Crashing on my feet

Disgorging their weight onto the sand

Becoming sand

I feel the fingers of the morning sun

Brushing my hair

As it wakes me up

I feel its warmth humming to me a new hope
every day

I feel it erupt in glee as I follow the path it
makes for me

I feel my eyes looking for him

In every face I see

In every plant

And bird

And human

In the songs I sing

And the words I read

In everything that I see

And I feel him not doing the same

And it's a tragedy I tell you

It's a tragedy

Not being enough for the person

Who is enough for you

It's a tragedy

Chasing a cloud that never stays in one place

And this paroxysm of hypersensitivity is a
curse

I like to dish out among my cronies

So they

For once

Believe me

When I say my head is a bottomless pit

That feeds on my hope

And devours it before I get to feel it

And that my head loves to move in circles

And pentagons

And hexagons

At the supermarket

In the water

Under the bed

Over the mountains

Into the grave

Finally, into the grave

And as much as I fancy death

I am sure all I'll be thinking about

During my final breaths

Is how I deserve to live more

And that death is one of those friends

Who won't put up a flashlight for you in the
dark

But will insist to arrange your entire wedding

Like I said

Always on the run

And this running has cost me

A decade of my good days

Cloaked in apprehension

Bathed in despair

While I scrimmaged for better ones

My feelings are a bunch of crossroads

And I am not sure which way to go

Because all the roads to my destiny

Are rendered sightless

By the storms raging in my head

The storms that I am ever ready to welcome
home

And they are not wrong when they say

I don't need an enemy

Because I am sufficient for myself

That death is just another word for how I live

If only

If only I could choose what to think

Before I could think

If only my thoughts weren't everywhere

And I wasn't such a mess

Then maybe there was hope

That someday

He will be mine

That someday

I would want to be mine too.

ANOREXIA NERVOSA

I am just a girl

All skin and bones

Who starves and moans,

A murky shadow behind a shadow

A filthy mask behind a mask,

Who tends to seek and feign normalcy in the
tundra of her madness,

If that's what they call it,

While there is none to be found,

Only a residuum of her ravaged desires,

Faintly hoping they still aspire

And an unattended funeral of her perished
self

And the broken bones of her amour propre,

Their barbed figures bruising her for life

Just like the thorny rigmaroles of body
shamers

Who mocked her for being divergent,

For being something she never chose to be,

For the identity she inwardly loathed

And for them, she wasn't anything near normal

So abnormal is what she became.

II – BREATHLESS MORTALS

"I see snippets of myself in other people. In their words and in their actions. Crumpled fragments that have built me up. Lost shreds that could have built me up. We are all one, divided by our stories, struggling to breathe through them."

MEA CULPA

This is an ode to the people I saw when I first
opened my eyes

To this uninviting hell of a world

Them holding onto me, me holding onto them

Them waiting for me to make some noise

Me waiting for them to shut up

Then finally, them smiling because me crying

This is for them who cheered when I took my
first step

And finished my first day at school

And then the last too

And graduated

And published my first book

And got married

And had kids

This is for them who never left my side

No matter how many sides I changed

This is for the ones who wiped my tears

When I fell off the stairs

Both literally and metaphorically

And they will probably be the only ones to
weep

When I finally depart

I think I will never know why I mentioned
them first here

Since I always used them as backup

Back when a little bit of indulgence still could
have mattered

But if this soupcon of honesty is the ignition
for my untold reparation

It isn't bad for a start

So, this is for them who took five steps
toward me

When I backed five

Who hugged me when I kept pushing them
away

Who lulled me to sleep when fear said,

'Good Morning, Deejay!'

To them, I want to say 'sorry'

Because I know I could have done better

If I had only tried harder

I know I could have just let my backlog of demons

Rot in that sepulchral heart of mine

Instead of cascading an abundance of my darkness

Over their light like a sorcerous cloak

I know I should have just let it go

When they couldn't see me for who I was

And what I was becoming

I know I should have understood and said 'it's okay'

When they told me I needed to do some explaining

About my mental state

Instead of running away

And hiding in my closet like it was all my fault

To them I want to say 'I love you'

Because I never did

Because I never could

Because I never tried

To them

I want to be a daughter

A sister

A friend

For freaking real this time

And this time,

And this time

When they call out my name

When they need me

When they miss me

I want to be there for them.

THE MISCONSTRUED DOLDRUMS

Emptiness is like holding a breath

You don't know you are holding

It's like attempting to fly without wings

Without will

It's like diving into a shallow pond of
freshwater lilies

That absorbs the ichor releasing from your
wounds

It's knowing you are happy

But not feeling it

It's knowing you are alive

But not believing it

It's every moment you want to cherish

But end up screwing even more

Because your joy is only a shadow of your
grief

Emptiness is such that you are bleeding all
over

By walking through a minuscule shaft

Covered in shards of glass

That pierce through your steel armor

Rich crimson blood trickles through the sole
of your feet

Where you tripped off a shard

Losing another one of your braces

Ouch, that hurt, but did it?

So, this is how you fall, you see?

Nobody pushes you off the edge of a cliff

Or doffs your feet off the ground in one swift
motion

You do that to yourself

Yes, you!

You choose to walk the difficile shaft taking
the others as too long

Too monotonous

You choose to hear the cacophony of
monsters

When the morning birds hymn to wake you
up

You choose to play gobbledygook

When there are hearts to be kept

Lives to be saved

Tears to be wiped

Don't get me wrong when I repeat you do that
to yourself

Because they are right when they say

You don't breathe by snitching breaths.

ELIXIR

This is an ode to the people I never took for granted

But lost them all the same

To the people I likened to the right side of my heart

That pumps oxygenated blood to my body

But they envenomed it with their insouciance

Bruised it with their travesty of affection

Then incapacitated it with a liniment they used as weapon

And named it friendship

Today, I want them all to know I have healed

That I survived the stones they hurled at me

When all I offered were tulips

That I forgive the blisters

Their words engraved on my shriveling heart

But I am still trying to forget

How loneliness popped all over my skin like smallpox

Simmered inside my heart and smelled like burning paper

And erupted from my brain

Like lava extravasating from a subterranean molten state

When they left me

I want them to know I was devastated

I had not planned a life without them

Now that they were gone

I didn't know who to look for

Whose names to call out

Whose jokes to laugh at

Whose calls to wait for

Whose voice to hear

Because I would be kidding myself if I said I had other friends

I didn't

I did have lackluster shadows though

That dwindled when I bellowed their names in the dark

That's how I knew they were never there

I am digging up old graves, yes,

But this time it's to articulate how strong I
have become

I have long lived with a mind that
scrimmages against its own self

Comminutes its own desires

Turns its own thoughts upside down

Over and over again

Until they lose meaning

And sagacity

Surely,

For a change,

I can handle a teeny bit of skirmish coming
from the outside

Can't I?

PINK SLIPS TO THE FLAWED

The new boutique at the end of my street

Breaks the ice with the catchphrase:

'The best are for the best,

So, enter this place only the best'

The lady at the salon across my
neighborhood

Says,

'We treat the flawless,

To breed the flawless"

My friend once told me it's easier to look
stupid than ugly

At least the former is your indiscretion

And while my brother is learning to say 'I am
ugly'

In Spanish

In German

And French

And Chinese

My father thinks learning is better done

In front of the mirror

What's funnier is

That last night my friends called me pretty

Lauding my dress

My jewelry

And the 'so on-point' makeup

That I cooed infamously

Ostended a malapert smile

And deflected the compliment with a flick of
my hair

Then I came home

Gave my caked face one jeering glance

And unpacked my scars one by one

Beginning with the thick cloud of untended
dissonance

Now rolling down my cheek in surrender

The irony of looking for perfection is that

This is our only flaw

We have spawned a measly world for our
children

Where acceptance is an abnegated identity

Where beauty is a white face

Be it caked with unearthly chemicals

Ravenous black hair

Big, brown eyes

5 ft. 10 inches of a fragile body

Unshaved arms and legs

Or wherever there's supposed to be
unnecessary hair

Long and smoothly filed nails with a
shimmering polish

And a people-face with a people-smile

Where love is a story mutated too many times
to make sense

Where bullying is just another word for
meaningful friendships

Where money can buy everything

But not respect

Respect solely for being the only ones

Like each other

To exist

To share a breath in this world

Nearing its last breath with every passing day

To be characters in the same story

And puppets of a single puppeteer

And as a compliant suburbanite of this
perfectionist realm,

I wonder what brought us here

And what has kept us in this prison of want

Where skin is the priciest jewelry

Yet something nobody likes to show off

Where people buy replicas to bury it

So they don't have to bother with muggers

Where revealing skin is a sin

The world deems unpardonable

While God looks down at us

Discerning who gave us the right

To pigeonhole his creation into preposterous
units

Enforcing a pirated manual of the mighty and
the weak

To establish his criteria of beauty

And perfection

He didn't feel necessitated to define

And how dare they circumscribe his favorite
color

His favorite gender

His favorite class

And sentence hell to anyone they didn't
understand

How dare they hatch rules about how to look

How to speak

What to wear

How to smile

When to cry

How to cry

How not to cry

How to breathe

When all he wanted from us

Was to be the best version of ourselves

He looks down at us,

More amused than chagrined,

Reckoning what a time it is to be alive

What a time it is to consider getting dressed
up

When the naked insides are rotting away

To consider gauging the specks and foibles of
people

When the inner child dies with neglect

What a time it is to smirch the hearts of each
other

When the soul languidly expires in its void of
courtesy

This place we live in

Is a dungeon for the faulty two-bits

For those who want to be all they can be

For those who choose the odds

Despite the odds

For those who refuse to give up their souls

To stand in the queue

There is no home for the needy

For the fragile

For the kind

For the beauteous hearts

To be a part of this pandemonium

You either hate

Or survive the hate.

AN ODE TO THE GRIEVERS OF MY SELF-ESTEEM

Writing is medicine for people who eat their own tongue

For those who trip over their own voice

And lose their marbles trying to expound their pain

To someone who doesn't want to know

Hell, it's a jog in the park for those who cannot climb the mountains

An art class for those who hate science

A rostrum for that guy who wanted to sing

But is stuck cramming medicine into his brain

That just wouldn't retain it

A mother to that dorky tongue-tied girl in class

Who couldn't tell her mother she was depressed

That last night she couldn't sleep

Because she wanted to be in her arms

Crying her lungs out to her

Which, in turn, was because some big kids in her neighborhood

Had told her she was fat

It's a fluky milestone for us fraidy cats

To own what could never be ours

To shamelessly call it some unrequited love

That we never fought for

That we never dared to approach

So don't mind me when I talk about love

Because when I talk about love

I don't mean love kinda love

Because when you really love something

You fight for it

Anyways,

I was blathering about how my words have treated me

Like my best friend never could

How they babysat me

Every time the world told me I wasn't enough

How they helped me touch the sky with my heart

And the moon with my sorrow

How they purloined the burden embedded on
my shoulders

Drop by drop

And doled it out among the grievers of my
self-esteem

I haven't let my heart forget the beauty of
that night

When I had asked my words to escape free

And wander into the wilderness of pages

That seemed to call out to the grief in me

To the unshed tears swarming my pen

To the darkness inhabiting my heart

And the sleepless nights now ringing my eyes

I let my eyes breathe in the perfection of my
pain

The manifestation of it

In the eyes of other people

When they found their souls on the pages

Where I had let the ink drink my sorrow

Devour it like the most scrumptious of its
cuisines

And honor the taste that followed

I wasn't about saying all I feel

So I killed my voice

Crushed it under my tongue

And decanted the vestiges

Into the ampoules of my backdoor emotions

With the apt label,

'All I will never say'

Sprinkling them,

Like salt to taste,

On my words

Just so I could become the voice of other
people

Drowning in the qualmish depths of what
they did

What they should

What they could

Just so I could become the antidote

To their paroxysms of sorrow

And the shredded cellophane

To fill their baskets of loneliness

Or the voids created by their cherished
fugitives

And ensure

With all my might and main

That my words are the door to their favorite
release

That my cries of woe are the gauze pads to
their wounds

That my tears are the chaperons to their
smiles

So they never have to keep an ampoule of
their own

So they never have to need a backdoor.

SYNONYMS FOR WRITING

Writing—

The unuttered apology

The anonymous well-wisher

The keeper of endless desires

And unkempt regrets

The selfless philanthropist

The unpaid nurse

The childless mother

And the orphan child

The specimens of a journey

And the journey itself

The benevolent master

The timid servant

The frightened dog

The determined lover

The jealous lover

The mighty lover

The silent lover

The boisterous lover

The dead lover

The lover

And his love

And his beloved

The friend in doom

And the sight in gloom

The anthem of victory

And that of joy

The inaudible tongue

The oversensitive ears

The unseeing eyes

The deadly arm

The paralyzed leg

The crude fear

The breathless breath

Writing—

My unshed tears

My broken smile

My favorite pillow

My ugly reality

My weeping hello

My breathless goodbye

My jittery confession

My adamant denial

My immortal grief

My galloping heartbeat

My breathless breath

Poetry—

My new name

My new name

My new name.

WHERE HUMANITY SNORES

To the world,

Kashmir is a gleaming sediment of struggle

A repercussion of self-determination

A war procreating another war

To them, it's a recrement of hedonism

And of greed disguised as humanity

To them, it's a bedtime story of beauty and
the two beasts

A pipe dream of its warmongering masters

A question mark on the map

A fissure in the peace of its mountains

A history with two sides

And no truth

Because those who know the truth

And see it

And live it

Have their mouths sealed

And their eyes pelleted

And their lives torn apart

Because those who know the truth

Have no say in it

And when they so much as dare to speak

The world goes blind

And deaf

And dead

To bat an eye on what happens next

So today

I want to speak for them

Today, I want the world to know that

My Kashmir is a heartbeat

And it pumps life into us

72 times per minute

My Kashmir is an echo of pain and strife

For a future so bright

It almost damaged our sight

My Kashmir is all the lives

We lost to freedom

And all the childhoods

We lost to war

My Kashmir is a tragedy so relentless

So unfading

Even the sky screams for change

It is all the darkness we have earned

And all the light we never deserved

I want to tell them that

My Kashmir is a breath we lost on our way
home

It is a lullaby for the orphans

Who never could uncover their crime

It is a deathbed for the naïve young boy

Who died protecting his sister

And for the mother who doesn't know

What happened to her kids

My Kashmir is the price you pay for raising
your voice

In a land where silence is the norm

But today,

It is time we tell them

That my Kashmir is not a rope for tug of war

They can keep pulling until it breaks

It is not a bubble wrap they can pop for fun

It is not a melody they can dance to

It is an echo they cannot cover their ears to

It is a voice that will not be subdued

And a life that will not be shattered anymore

It is time we tell them that

If the meaning of Pakistan is La ilaha Illallah

Then we are all soldiers

And we are all martyrs

And we are all Kashmir.

MATRIARCHAL INANITION

Women in my family think the word 'no' is cursed

And as the profanity creeds suggest

Curses only seem credible coming from the right mouth

And the right mouth for this word

Knows it belongs to them

In our mouths

This word

This curse

Settles like the tip of a dagger

So when we so much as dare to speak

It pricks and pricks

Until we bleed compliance

Until our tongues are too scarred

To form the right words

Until 'I'll figure it out'

Replaces

'No way'

Until 'Sorry' blurts out

Before we garner the courage to say

'How dare you?'

Until we are robbed off the nerve

To lock horns

Over the sun that must also bless our lands
with its light

And canopies that should be ours in the first
place

Until we learn to give up all our lights

For darkness that blinds us

So we don't get to thwart the fists that come
at us

And who needs a canopy

Where there is never any light?

So we stand bare

Under the watchful sky

With only the moon kind enough

To bestow its light on those we ought to trust

On those who show us the path

Even if they are lost in their own journey

Those who glow the brightest

In our darkness

Who make sure we get to see the sunrise

After every sepulchral night

But

We women

You see

Pay a price for everything

For our struggles and our victories

For our tears and our smiles

For our dreams and our delusions

Nothing

I tell you

Nothing

That comes to us

Is for free

Even the air that we breathe

Reeks of misogyny

So strong

So mighty

One can sniff the dreams that could never be
seen

And the smiles that never could reach the
eyes

And the bodies that once held sanctuaries
inside of it

But are now tombs of trust

And mercy

And childhoods lost to sins not known

Not understood

And the bodies that

At the end of the day

Were just bodies

And not a soul-protecting combination

Of flesh and skin

Not a public interest record of the food we eat

And how we eat

And how much we eat

And if we eat at all

The problem with our gender is that

It is watched from all angles

But seen from none

And while we have a lot to say

We don't have much say

In what we have to say

So we run

As fast as we can

As long as we can

And hide our skins

In all the places we can

And try not to remember the whereabouts

Of every piece lost

Because remembering our frittered proprium

Makes us want to do something about it

Which doesn't help

If the anesthetized spirits of your kind

Keep pulling you back

In the same water they once drowned in

Where lie the last crumbs

Of their once embraced vehemence

And not being able to do anything

Eats away

At the hope

That we drizzle on our bodies every morning

So,

You will find a piece of us everywhere

In everything

But never all of it

Never in one place

We are a broken frame

Lost in the sea

Never to be found

Never to be fixed

Even though the picture inside floats
somewhere

Shipshape

Unscathed

And because love says

You don't choose the parts you want to love

You either love or you don't

Even if it's your own damn self

Scattered in the water

We tend to forget about that too

But men won't get that, would they?

Do they know what pouring from an empty
cup feels like?

Is it humanly possible for them

To walk in the shoes of someone

Who has stopped walking?

Or someone

Who has never tried to walk in the first
place?

We are players

In an absurd

And unscrupulous game

Scampering to get to the roof of a building

And lift the flag of victory

While the opponents are already on the roof

With the flag in their hands

This game of life

As we call it

Is pretty messed up

Because we women

Will be mothers and daughters and sisters

And single and married and widowed

And pregnant and infertile

Before we can be anything

We will be short

And weak

And grumpy

And fat

And clingy

And needy

And dark

And sexy

And asking for it

Anything but ourselves

Always

Always

Seen

And understood

Through the eyes of others

Always borrowing an identity

From the men in our lives

But men

Will simply

Be men

By all means

Irrespective of their flaws

And quirks

And crimes

Of the personality traits they so love

Of the people they hold close to their hearts

And of everything beyond their control

And yet

In a world that thinks we do not need anyone

Because we are so full of ourselves

We do need someone

Who can see through all the labels

At the woman heaving inside of us

Waiting to be saved

At the girl that grew up too soon

At the daughter who learned to shut her
mouth

When there were men talking

At the sister who once dreamed

To be greater than her brother's honor

We are all here

Too gullibly hopeful to shed a tear

If you are willing to look

And touch

And heal

We have been told to wait for you,

You

Who would see us for who we are

Ever since we were young girls

With unscratched souls

If you are nearby

Please pay a visit.

THE MULTIVERSE - Inspired by Blake Crouch's Dark Matter

As I say, I wish it were true

The very many stories of you

You are one, but you are many

You are pure, but you are canny

In some, you live to outshine the world

In others, your strings are loose

But no,

You might not want to see all the different shades of you

Their life being a devastated facsimile of yours

You are a tree with endless branches

Where parts of you yearn to be one

You are but a plethora of de trop and cherished decisions

Where figments of your failure float ceaselessly

And there are still the remnants of what could have been

In a sea of perennial choices

Where you chase the multiverse

For a version of you

With no perturbing regrets

Only a schema of perfection

But this infraction has cost you a life

A life of your exemplary self

And you have failed a million versions of you

In a million different ways

So does your absurd self still relish the forged
victory?

TOPSY-TURVIED

I want to write something about the way

My hope left me wheezing

At the portcullis of sorrow

When my mother was diagnosed with cancer

Just when my freshly procured field of happiness

Was all I could think about

Just when my heart had become friends with my wounds

As it warbled the verses of healing

Day and night

In fight and fright

About the way I witnessed the remnants of it

Simmering atop the palpable odds

Of never seeing her healthy again

Of never seeing her smile brighten up my day

On days

When the sun refused to rise on my side

Of not being there when she needed me the most

I am aware of the blue devils

Now crawling their way down my spine

As my words keep chucking me

Out of my head

By fits and starts

As the weight

Long since enshrined into my soul

Bleeds through my eyes

And the pain hoarded in my heart

Like leftover food

Becomes stale

Death

I believe

Must only be death

For the dead

If they can snitch our breaths

And walk away

Without ever looking back

But a sempiternal trauma

For those left behind

Forever glued to their fleeting existence

Forever ruminating

How their love couldn't be enough to save
them

How their love never could reach the right
heart

And the apology that never clicked home

Today she is alive

Today she is breathing

But God knows

I have been gasping for air

Since the day

Her illness clutched my flimsy heart

And my body forgot how to pretend a normal

When my insides were on public display

How not to act like

The fear brining me to my knees

Was merely a slapstick comedy

And my mouth

A tundra of all the words

Gone sour with disuse

I am tired of dodging a volley of grisly
scenarios

And running over

To my Siberian self for refuge

When nothing helps

Trust me

The cold does

And I am not a warmth freak anyway

So Maybe I am not a language maestro

With a stockpile of schmaltzy words

Plastered to my grief

And ideally hand-packed

With a bonus 'fragile' sticker

To meet the emotional needs

Of someone who is yet to choose

Between aging and fading

Maybe I am not an off-the-record telepathist

Who knows when to help

Or a lovey-dovey attendant

Who insists to stay

At all costs

Maybe my face doesn't emanate

'Always available' vibes

When people attempt to read it

Because let's be honest

I have been trying to read myself for years

And I still don't know

When or if I ever got it right

Pardon me for being off-track

But hey,

That's who I am

A busted bag of bones

Always in the midst of facilitating
negotiations

And contriving ceasefires

To the civil wars

In my body

To pay any attention

To the bloodshed outside it

But if there's one thing

That remains unscathed to date

In my ravaged reality

Is that I am a part of her

Her body atrophied its flesh

To give me life

In a world

Where you already have a 50% chance of
living

Considering all the breathing rights are
inscribed for men here

That too with us being our only enemies on
the planet

And also that her pain sojourns in my body

Like a soaring pulse

Every time she refuses to acknowledge it

Always, always forgetting

That she breathes inside of me

That her pain leaves an echo in my body

As a tribute to my time in her womb

And if I weren't such a hysterical freak

And if my words

And my grief

Weren't so bald

I would share with her

Some of the hope

That I salvaged from intermittent bouts

Of accidental happiness

To be used in my emotional exigencies

The hope that keeps me sane on most days

And lulls me to sleep

In the voice of my mother

And if I weren't myself

If I could be anything

But myself

I would be the ground that she treads

And the air that she breathes

So I would always have a way back to her.

III- PARAMOUR

"Things have to go really, really wrong before they go right. Darkness must first overwhelm before it can be underwhelmed. And tears must first stain your cheeks before they can calm your heart.

So here's to the right things

And to the right person

And to the darkness that gave way to this light

And to the tears I lost and the smiles that I gained

Here's to the good days,

To him

And to us."

HEARTSORE

To him

I am just another girl

Emotive and scrimpy

Wispy and puerile

A sight worthless for His Majesty

Relative to the beauty that entertains him

But I doubt he can really see me

Through the wall of adamant that separates
us

Through the mask that I am inclined to wear

Beyond which is a girl who yearns for him

Wailing and whimpering under the burden of
her lamenting heart

Sometimes clouting against the invisible wall

Shouting his name that is a dysphoric music
to her ears

If only he could see

Could hear

Could know the torment his eyes are to my
eyes

His voice is to my ears

His smile is to my fracturing heart

If only I could break myself into smithereens

For him to see his name on every minuscule
fragment

If only I had the courage to make him look

Look what I have done to my innocent self

And what he did to my myriad of emotions

That were once mortal

To my ocean of desires that keeps desiccating

Until one day there would only be a drop left,

His name glistening on it loftily,

Imprisoning me with no key to freedom

But what would he care if he knew?

What does it even matter?

For I knew the first time I saw him,

Fell for him,

That he was impossible,

That we were impossible.

WHITE FLAG

I just want to see him

One last time

Feel his eyes on me

Even if they are not feverishly melting in my
love

Even if they are not meant to be there in the
first place

And I want to see his lips parting

And his smile widening in response to my
attempted joke

I want him to ruffle his rumpled hair

And walk like the wraith that he always did

Maybe God wasn't too kind to grant me a
forever with him

I am too unfortunate to wish for it

And too weak to ask for it

And too insufficient for the entirety of him

Too ugly

Too short

Too stupid

But I deserve this one last reunion

One last smile

That one last inside joke

Be it an excuse to make me grieve for him
later

No, I am not seeking another unlikely chance

I don't even care if there is one

Because really, what does it matter?

All I care about is that one last sight of him

Not a forever

Not everything

But something

Anything

I promise then,

It won't happen again

I promise then,

I will try my best

To make that last sight of him

My forever.

STARGAZER

When I said,

Writing is medicine for people who eat their own tongue

For those who trip over their own voice

And lose their marbles trying to expound their pain

To someone who doesn't want to know

And that,

It's a fluky milestone for us fraidy cats

To own what could never be ours

To shamelessly call it some unrequited love

That we never fought for

That we never dared to approach.

I meant to be writing about him

But my brave, brave penning knees gave out

And I had to stop

I had to stop

Because *this* is the right time to tell him

That he was the right one

That I so hysterically wished for him to be the
right one

When he was all but a ruse my mind played
me into

A plangent cacophony that kept caterwauling
in my ears

Hideously synchronized with the rhythm

Of my pitter-pattering heart

A crevasse I kept plunging into

Knowing it might freeze me to death

The end of a heart fluttering for another heart

An abysmal ocean I voluntarily chose to pull
me under

And choke my lungs

Until I stopped screaming which couldn't be
heard

So this one is for him

Who had no idea I missed him

When the nights became too murky

Too sequestered

And the moon provided no comfort

And during the day

When the sun became so hungry

It ate my tongue

When its puncturing light became too bright
for my sight

I didn't know which way to look so I could
plead

So I could plead my spunk back

I missed him when the fairytales I kept
reading ad infinitum

Concluded with a happily ever after

And my eyes sang his name

Until the pages wept

I missed him when my name in his
lampooning voice

And his adorable laugh

Infiltrated my ears

Like molten glass crawling through skin

Years later, he still has no idea

That he had given me the cancer of lily-
livered love

The herpes of unreciprocated caring

The psychological disorder characterized by
the inability

And an indisposition to forget a certain
person

And a pig-headed arm

That refused to pluck out an arrow-headed
memory

From the heart

That stuck like gum

But stung like acid

Not to mention the resounding hollow his
absence had left

And a pair of plain-vanilla, prosaic eyes

That would bleed for a glimpse of him

And I healed

I healed despite the odds that said:

'You only love once'

And now that I have healed

I want him to see me claim my victory over
his memories

That are pulling away from me

Like tides gone feeble through distance

Like dead skin leisurely wearing away

I want to make a headlong eye contact with
him

Now that it's easier to look into his eyes

And not have the sapphire glow of the night
sky staring back

Or feel his eyes flicker

Like a million glittering stars falling to earth

Diving into an ocean as dark as the color of
my own eyes

I want to look into his eyes

Eyes that never could see me

And tell him

That I do not love him

That I do not love him

And that I never did

And when I have done so

I hope,

I hope I believe my own words

Level my chin

Cobble up my spine

And walk away.

GRATUS ANIMUS

I had a life before you too

If you call it so

A misconjectured,

Loused up realm of my very existence

A frippery of rickety pride

An amalgamation of half-baked desires

And dreams gone wrong

So very wrong

In a world encompassing dark and dingy
nights,

Cold and jittery lights,

I fought and fought for a mere piece of this
macrocosm

For a sliver of hope

In this overawing abode we call society

Where I was throttled by people

Who claimed to possess me

And know me

When I don't know myself

They dug wells for me and threw me in

For a charge as low as my rarity

I wasn't one of them

But that doesn't mean I never wanted to
become one

So I kept fighting,

Fighting the wrong person,

If I might add

All spite and fright aimed inwardly

At the woman who deserved love and
adulation

Cradling and satiation

For what she endured

Despite her petty, ignoramus self

You see,

I never had a chance in this mundane world

But I begetted one

And kept it safe in the empyreal wings of my
heart

Until I was able to transfer the contents

Of my hope-filled vials

Into a valise

Hundreds and thousands of them

And carry it everywhere I went

Like a hard-earned trophy,

A memento of my courage

And resilience

And fidelity to everything that wasn't mine

But still mine in every respect

They killed me in a way flowers die

When they are plucked and trodden over

Their beauty and fragrance languidly fading
away

Such that they become what eyes never want
to see,

Noses never want to smell

Yes, this is what I used to be—

A disintegrated petal at the bottom of a
wilting plant

But you see

There were eyes that saw me lying at death's
door

Where I pounded with bruised knuckles

Bellowed with a ruptured larynx

All that for the sake of freedom I couldn't put
into words

But they saw

And heard

And heeded

Spilling new seeds on my carrion

All the while chanting exuberant notes of
reawakening

I gobbled up those seeds

Drunk high on their words and rose

And bloomed

And boomed

That's when you came

And saw what I never was

Saw what I had spent years believing

Was impossible for me to become

Saw what they had done to me

In their hullabaloos for perfection

Saw how many crimes,

How many sins went unpunished

How many wounds remained wounds

Even after they had healed

You liberated the vials of hope I had kept
clutched to my chest

Let them go free in the air

So I could breathe

And swim

And dance in their glory

And you embraced the truths carrying the
bulk of my weight

You embraced who I was

And who I had become

Without ever complaining what it was like

To see me covered in undeserved scars

I hated wearing like armor on my steeled skin

And above all,

You made me love you

Because you made me love me

And loving,

As a universal rule,

Must, must begin on the inside

For it to grow on the outside

So if my soul was miffed by a myriad of
qualms before you

A bedlam of raging storms

And torrents that threatened to extirpate my existence

Your soul calmed them all with a mere confession of love;

Love,

Which I had so selfishly,

So amateurishly defined as a superficial sentiment

A sentiment

I was made to believe

Did not thrive on the inside

So thank you, my love

Thank you

For redefining a word

That had lost its meaning to me

All over again.

HEALING WAR-BUILT HANDS: THE POST-WAR ORDEAL

I wonder if it's possible to fix me

To put back the dismembered,

Haywire pieces of my spunk

Brick by brick

Into the void that is my soul

And still not make them look like

Stitches on a sulphurous wound

Apocryphal,

Esoteric spells on my star-crossed sanity,

Or a webbed-glass wall frame

Topsy-turvy on a skewed nail

Still there because no one cares enough to replace it

I have scruples about the contingency of it all

Because I am not sure if I am still alive

If it's those last moments before the final quietus

That I am scaring up

My shallow breaths bubbling

Like the ebullient volcano of Mount Vesuvius

My heart racing against the odds

400 times per minute

A brisk right,

A too close left,

Then a precariously incurvating U-turn

Seemingly ready to crash into a tree bark and
break its neck

Yeah, tachycardia serves me right

I loved running away, anyways, didn't I?

If I could, I would give up this translucent
offal of a skin

For something more fuliginous

Sooner than its natural, rhythmic
disintegration

For something that knows how to shine

Despite the darkness

For something that knows how to give

Despite the hollow within

For something that knows how to love

And love

And love

Despite all the hate

If I could, I would venture the gloom within
my soul

And lighten it up with all the candles

You gifted me on my birthday

That I never used

Yes, I am sorry

My world is still too dark for the light that
you bring

I am sorry,

My world is blown too many times to resettle

I am sorry I am not the beginning

Or the end you expect me to be

I have lost too many times to count,

To expect victory

You don't know what it's like

To finally have a thing you have wished for all
your life

And then watch as it grows florets of hope
within you

That prick at your maimed skin

And seduce you with their beguiling odor

Because really,

How long can they last?

So next time I tell you

I am a hopeless plight

A darkened sight

A punctured kite

Do not run into me giving excuses for your
mythical failure

Or tell me you are going to fix me

Because now you know,

Now you know

It's not a wish that could be materialized

What you need to tell me is that

Baby,

Broken is cool

Broken is beautiful

Broken is perfect

Broken is whole

And that it's better to be a flawed whole

Than a flawless half

Tell me it's the latest trend

The fanciest garment in the market

Tell me it's the cheekiest vogue

Tell me I am okay

And that it's okay to not be okay

Because okay itself will never be completely
okay

Tell me all that and keep telling me

And I will believe you

I swear I will

Or at least

I will give my best.

LOVE LETTER

You are stupid

And funny

And so very annoying

I hate you

But I also love you

I love you so much

You keep wanting to hear me say these 3
magical words

But they hold no meaning for me

For what I hold for you in my heart

Is much, much greater than what your ears
can hear

What your heart can bear

For the butterflies that you send fluttering in
my stomach

Are a lot more significant

Than the words I do not

Would not

Cannot summon

And speak

Without embarrassing myself

Without feeling guilty for scoring you so low
in my heart

I am not about saying all I feel

You know as much from what little I have
told you about myself

But what I never told you is that you are
beautiful

Infinitely beautiful

Not in a way most people are

You are beautiful to the core of your heart

And even deeper

To the pits of your soul

I love you

The only colors you love are black and white

And yet you fill my life with a million different
colors

In a million different ways

You hate yellow

And that's stupid

Because who hates yellow?

Yellow is the color of peace

The color of comely smiles and laughter

And friendships

It is the color of innocence

And well, if I were a color,

I would be yellow

But excuse me,

That's an anecdote

I intend to broach later

So yeah, if I were a color

I would be yellow

Not that it's my favorite color

My favorite color is blue

The color of bravery

And courage

And audacity

The color of calming oceans and morning
skies

I am all but a stranger to which

Yet I love having the blues of not being with
you sometimes

Oh look, how the narcissistic in me

Changed the topic again

So what I wanted to say was

That I love you

More than words can say

And I am sorry I lied when I said I hate you

You know that, right?

I am sorry I was being freakish when I
pushed you away

And told you that you have hurt me

You are the embrocation to my antediluvian
wounds

I am sorry I was being a poophead

When I bantered I am not yours

I am yours in every way possible

Like stars are to the night sky

Like water is to the oceans

Like fries are to me

Like books are to me

Like you are to me

Like you are to me

Like you are to me

For the entirety of our existence

Till death do us apart

And we become nothing but a disseminated
memory

In the shallows of someone's heart

In the gloom of a cemetery

In the melancholy of our woebegone families

And when we are resurrected to meet our
fates in the afterlife

I will look for you

I will look for you

I will look for you

And ask for you

And have you by my side when I enter
Heaven.

UNSCHOOLED

They ask me if I am happy

If his advent is the miracle I had been waiting for

The boulevard to a cure,

Which I wonder why they still believe exists

And when I say 'I don't know'

Because I really don't

They convince me that I am

That I am

And that my face

My rubescent cheeks

My effervescent smile

Are all a peachy reflection of his love

When love is a transplant organ

My body rejected more than twice

When love is a book I decided not to have on my bookshelf

But kept it all the same

When love is a dance party for the highfalutins

And I am a homespun shrimp

Who doesn't know how to dance

They ask me if there is ever going to be a
happy ending

For a person like me,

Me, a long-faced existential bloke

With a thing for self-destruction

If I will ever stop joking about death

Like it's my sweetest guilty pleasure

The last time I asked myself this question

My nerves rattled with shame

And my eyes shoved the electrolytes off them

In spurts of fury

I wish there was a way

To dismantle the skyscraping architecture of
hope

Where lies the mortal replica of my Eden

Refashioned for the hundredth time

For newly arriving intimates

Bathed in uncensored,

Unrestrained chagrin and rubrics

And the citadel of dreams

That refuses to crumble

Under the squandering weight of reality

So, I ask them

When was the last time the sun transformed

To adjust to the moon's darkness

And when has the moon ever not existed
during the day?

I ask them why do the caterpillars,

In their most fragile state,

Do not need their other halves to turn into
butterflies?

And how can a lion in the wilderness

Be the sole gerent of the animal kingdom

And not need a partner?

I ask them why does a woman need a man

To be whole

To be happy

When he doesn't need her

To be whole

To be happy?

How can the world expect so much happiness
from A woman

Who is sucked dry by the fangs of patriarchy

Whose beatitude is a broken cage

Whose freedom is a repercussion of soul
euthanasia?

How does the world then expect fruits from a
tree

That wasn't doused in its essentials for
years?

But I also long to tell them

That his love is like paradise on fire

Like moon during the day

And stars a million miles away from reach

His love is an unfinished prayer

And gratitude unobserved

And a childhood dream misunderstood

What I mean to say is that

He is a rococo mansion in downtown

I cannot afford to live in

And a Lamborghini I don't know how to drive

He is the sky

And the stars

And the darkness beyond

He is the parallel to my dreams

The mirror image of my harbored ideals

He is light and darkness

He is thunder and the calm after it

He is everything and nothing

All in one body

All of which is mine

Mine

And how nightmarish it sounds

To own a thing

Much less a person

When you can't own yourself

When you can't walk the earth

Without staggering on your own two feet

When your breath feels home in someone
else's mouth

When, in a room full of people,

You are the only person you find awful

And how evil could you be

To want love from a person

You can't love back

Because love is still a skill

You forgot to practice inside the fence

So this one is for him

Whose love I can't cherish

Because of all the wrong lessons I learnt
about love

Whose love is sunshine in its purest form

Scorching but ethereal

But all I ever wanted was rain

Not knowing that rain could be acidic

This is for him,

My love,

Who stepped into my life

When I had exited my own

Who took my hand

When I pulled it away

And held it till I wept

And spilled my reality

Over his heart

This is for the man who regressed into a boy

And who laughed like a maniac

Just so I would stop crying

And for the man who cried with me

And shared all my pain

I, for once, wasn't there for myself

When I hoped others would be

And you see,

This is where I went wrong

Because I expected love

To taste like my favorite chocolate

Sickly sweet and moonstruck

Like pardoned sins and decoded quandaries

Like baby sleep

And first steps

But when love came around

It was bitter

And tasted like unsweetened cocoa

And reeked of blotted out memories

With tails that carved out shadows from my
sins

It felt like a leap over my balcony

With no one to stop me from falling

When love came around

I had to stop walking,

Stop running

Not because it was all I had been looking for

But because it was all I had been running
from

It's uncanny

Because I knew what I wanted

And still chose him

And would choose him in all other worlds

That are to come

If they are to come

It's uncanny because there has never been a
shred of doubt

For a person with pathological indecisiveness

Hell, it's incredible

Because I found love where I wasn't looking

And kept it

And cradled it

And watched it grow

With every passing day

I built my own greenhouse with his love

And promenaded inside

A synthetic show of my courage

And watched the thorns below the roses

Turn to ash under my feet

One by one

And even though my eyes burned

With the ash winging inside of them

I let my mouth spew the fable

Which had colored my teeth to yellow

And singed my tongue to onyx;

'He is the one',

Over and over again

Like a playlist on repeat

And a war nearing defeat

For a stubborn heartbeat.

ACKNOWLEDGEMENTS

To the people who look at the stars and wish.

To the stars who listen and the dreams that are answered   ~ Sarah J. Maas

My dreams have been very kind to me. Their mere existence have led me through so many trials, and have held me tight when I thought failure was inevitable. There were days when I forgot about them, or at least pretended to forget about them so I didn't have to worry about fulfilling them, but even on those days, they shined bright at the back of my heart, always, always smiling, reminding me of hope. So a big thanks goes to my dreams, for simply being mine.

And the credit of their existence goes to Allah, my best friend, my armour, my light. The dreams he showered me with, have kept me alive. When light left my heart, these dreams gave me hope of better days because there is always a morning to every dark night. So this book is for him who didn't leave me alone when even I wasn't there for myself.

Another huge thanks is for my family; my rock. My mother, Arifa Adhia, she is my sunshine in human form and her countless prayers and smiles have made me who I am today. Please never stop praying for me. My father, G. Mohiuddin Adhia, is my hero, my ideal. It is from him that I have learned how to pursue my goals, no matter how difficult they may seem. I grew up seeing him run after his goals and I am so so proud of him because he never gave up. It is from him that I have learnt hardwork, and perseverence. Mama and papa, thank you for always treating my dreams as yours. This is for you. I hope I make you proud.

And then comes my pack of sweet and sours; my sisters, Rabia Adhia and Umaima Adhia. I know how different and sometimes distant I have been from you two, but you both never left my side. Thank you for always being there when I needed you and for always adding a bit of spice and life to my dead soul.

He may be the last one of my family members I am mentioning here, but in no way is he any less. He might not be a fan of books, but this man is the reason I am writing this today. My husband, Mustufa Munaf, is a gem and I am so lucky to have someone who believes my dreams are important enough to be turned into reality. Thank you, my love, I owe this to you in so many ways.

I also want to thank my friends; Soha Ahmed, Tooba Anis, Ramsha Sajid, Ayesha Farooq and Adeena Mansoor for seeing a writer in me, and for believing this was possible. Thank you for reading my poems and giving me the feedback that I needed when I couldn't find anyone. Your constructive criticism has always helped me.

Printed and Bound by *Passive Printers* - www.passiveprinters.com
Printing press that offers Print on Demand (POD) Facility.
Printed in The Islamic Republic of Pakistan.